W9-BAE-357

Contents

Decadent & Delicious

¾ cup all-purpose flour

¾ cup NESTLÉ® TOLL HOUSE® Baking Cocoa

¼ teaspoon salt

½ cup (1 stick) butter, cut into pieces

½ cup granulated sugar

½ cup packed brown sugar

3 large eggs, *divided*

2 teaspoons vanilla extract

1 cup chopped pecans

¾ cup NESTLÉ® TOLL HOUSE® Premier White Morsels

½ cup caramel ice cream topping

¾ cup NESTLÉ® TOLL HOUSE® Semi-Sweet Chocolate Morsels

PREHEAT oven to 350°F. Grease 8-inch-square baking pan.

COMBINE flour, cocoa and salt in small bowl. Beat butter, granulated sugar and brown sugar in large mixer bowl until creamy. Add *2 eggs,* one at a time, beating well after each addition. Add vanilla extract; mix well. Gradually beat in flour mixture. Reserve ¾ *cup* batter. Spread *remaining* batter into prepared baking pan. Sprinkle nuts and white morsels over batter. Drizzle caramel topping over top. Beat *remaining* egg and *reserved* batter in same large bowl until light in color. Stir in semi-sweet morsels. Spread evenly over caramel topping.

BAKE for 30 to 35 minutes or until center is set. Cool completely in pan on wire rack. Cut into bars.

Makes 16 brownies

Buckeye Cake

Cake
- 2 large eggs
- 1¼ cups granulated sugar
- ¾ cup all-purpose flour
- 6 tablespoons unsalted butter, melted
- 3 packets (1 ounce *each*) NESTLÉ® TOLL HOUSE® CHOCO BAKE® Pre-Melted Unsweetened Chocolate Flavor
- ½ teaspoon vanilla extract
- ⅛ teaspoon salt

Peanut Butter Layer
- ¾ cup creamy peanut butter
- ¼ cup unsalted butter, softened
- ¼ teaspoon vanilla extract
- ¾ cup powdered sugar

Ganache
- 1 cup heavy whipping cream
- 2 cups (12-ounce package) NESTLÉ® TOLL HOUSE® Semi-Sweet Chocolate Morsels
- ⅓ cup NESTLÉ® TOLL HOUSE® Peanut Butter & Milk Chocolate Morsels

PREHEAT oven to 350°F. Grease 9-inch-round cake pan. Line bottom of pan with parchment paper; grease.

For Cake

COMBINE eggs and sugar in large bowl. Stir in flour, melted butter, Choco Bake, vanilla extract and salt until smooth. Pour into prepared pan.

BAKE for 25 minutes or until a wooden pick inserted in the middle comes out clean. Cool on wire rack for 5 minutes. Run knife around edge of cake; cool for an additional 10 minutes. Invert cake onto serving platter. Remove pan and parchment; cool completely.

For Peanut Butter Layer

BEAT peanut butter, butter and vanilla extract in medium mixer bowl until combined. Gradually beat in powdered sugar. Spread mixture on cake. Refrigerate for 30 minutes.

For Ganache

HEAT cream in small saucepan to boiling; remove from heat. Add semi-sweet morsels; let stand 5 minutes. Stir; refrigerate for 30 minutes or until mixture is spreadable. Spread chocolate on top and sides of cake.

MICROWAVE peanut butter & milk chocolate morsels in resealable plastic bag on MEDIUM-HIGH (70%) power for 30 seconds. Knead bag to mix. If necessary, microwave at additional 10- to 15-second intervals until melted. Cut small hole from corner of bag; squeeze to drizzle over cake. Store in refrigerator. Let stand for 30 minutes before serving.

Makes 8 servings

Margarita Pie

Crust

- 1 cup crushed mini pretzels
- 6 tablespoons melted butter
- 1 tablespoon granulated sugar

Filling

- 2 tablespoons boiling water
- 1 envelope (7 grams) unflavored gelatin
- 1 can (12 fluid ounces) NESTLÉ® CARNATION® Evaporated Milk
- 1 cup granulated sugar
- 2 teaspoons grated lime peel
- ½ cup (4 to 5 medium limes) lime juice
- 1 teaspoon grated orange peel
- 2 tablespoons orange juice or orange-flavored liqueur
- 1 tablespoon tequila (optional)
- 2 cups frozen whipped topping, thawed, *divided*

   Coarse sanding sugar, fresh lime slices (optional)

For Crust

PREHEAT oven to 375°F. Combine pretzel crumbs, butter and sugar in 9-inch deep-dish (4-cup volume) pie plate. Press crumb mixture onto bottom and upsides of pie plate.

BAKE for 5 to 7 minutes or until lightly browned. Cool completely on wire rack

For Filling

PLACE gelatin in small bowl; stir in water. Let stand for 1 minute. Heat evaporated milk, sugar and softened gelatin in small saucepan over medium heat, stirring until sugar is dissolved and mixture is hot (do not boil). Pour into medium bowl. Refrigerate uncovered for 30 minutes until cool to touch. Add lime peel, lime juice, orange peel, orange juice and tequila; mix well. Gently whisk in 1 cup whipped topping. Pour into prepared pie crust.

REFRIGERATE for 2 hours or until set. Pipe remaining 1 cup whipped topping around edge of pie. Sprinkle whipped topping border with coarse sugar. Garnish with lime slices.

Makes 8 servings

Tips:

- 3 cups (4 ounces) mini pretzels will be needed to get 1 cup crushed.

- To save time, you may substitute a store-bought 10-inch (9-ounce) graham cracker crumb crust for pretzel pie shell.

- If you do not own a pastry bag, a resealable, heavy-duty plastic bag can be used. Cut corner of bag and pipe out whipped topping as desired.

Zesty Lemon Pound Cake

1 cup (6 ounces) NESTLÉ® TOLL HOUSE® Premier White Morsels

2½ cups all-purpose flour

1 teaspoon baking powder

½ teaspoon salt

1 cup (2 sticks) butter, softened

1½ cups granulated sugar

2 teaspoons vanilla extract

3 large eggs

3 to 4 tablespoons freshly grated lemon peel (about 3 medium lemons)

1⅓ cups buttermilk

1 cup powdered sugar

3 tablespoons fresh lemon juice

PREHEAT oven to 350°F. Grease and flour 10-cup Bundt pan.

MELT morsels in medium, uncovered, microwave-safe bowl on MEDIUM–HIGH (70%) power for 1 minute; STIR. Morsels may retain some of their original shape. If necessary, microwave at additional 10- to 15-second intervals, stirring just until morsels are melted. Cool slightly.

COMBINE flour, baking powder and salt in small bowl. Beat butter, granulated sugar and vanilla extract in large mixer bowl until creamy. Beat in eggs, one at a time, beating well after each addition. Beat in lemon peel and melted morsels. Gradually beat in flour mixture alternately with buttermilk. Pour into prepared Bundt pan.

BAKE for 50 to 55 minutes or until wooden pick inserted into cake comes out clean. Cool in pan on wire rack for 10 minutes. Combine powdered sugar and lemon juice in small bowl. Make holes in cake with wooden pick; pour *half* of lemon glaze over cake. Let stand for 5 minutes. Invert onto plate. Make holes in top of cake; pour *remaining* glaze over cake. Cool completely before serving.

Makes 12 to 16 servings

LIBBY'S® Pumpkin Pear Strudel

2 cups (about 2 small) peeled, cored and diced pears

1 cup LIBBY'S® 100% Pure Pumpkin

¾ cup packed brown sugar

¾ cup chopped walnuts

1 teaspoon ground cinnamon

⅛ teaspoon ground cloves

⅛ teaspoon ground ginger

2 sheets (17¼-ounce package) frozen puff pastry, thawed according to package directions, *divided*

1 large egg, lightly beaten

Cinnamon-sugar

PREHEAT oven to 375°F.

COMBINE pears, pumpkin, sugar, nuts, cinnamon, cloves and ginger in medium bowl. Spoon *one-half* of filling in center third of *1* pastry sheet.

MAKE downward slanting strips in outer sections of pastry (¾-inch apart) starting about 1 inch away from top of pastry and side of filling, cutting to outside edges. Starting at top, alternately fold left and right side pastry strips over filling forming a braid. Seal at top and bottom of strudel. Place on ungreased rimmed baking sheet. Repeat with *remaining* filling and pastry sheet. Brush strudels with egg; sprinkle with cinnamon-sugar.

BAKE for 25 to 30 minutes or until golden brown and puffy. Serve warm.

Makes 10 servings

Raisin Apple Bread Pudding

4 cups white bread cubes

1 medium apple, chopped

1 cup raisins

2 large eggs

1 can (12 fluid ounces) NESTLÉ® CARNATION® Evaporated Milk

½ cup Apple NESTLÉ® JUICY JUICE® All Natural 100% Juice

½ cup granulated sugar

1½ teaspoons ground cinnamon

Caramel ice cream topping (optional)

PREHEAT oven to 350°F. Grease 11×7-inch baking dish.

COMBINE bread, apple and raisins in large bowl. Beat eggs in medium bowl. Stir in evaporated milk, Juicy Juice, sugar and cinnamon; mix well. Pour egg mixture over bread mixture, pressing bread into milk mixture; let stand for 10 minutes. Pour into prepared baking dish.

BAKE for 40 to 45 minutes or until set and apples are tender. Serve warm with caramel topping.

Makes 8 servings

Chocolate Chip Cheesecake

Crust
- 1½ cups (about 15) crushed chocolate sandwich cookies
- 2 tablespoons butter or margarine, melted
- 2 cups (12-ounce package) NESTLÉ® TOLL HOUSE® Semi-Sweet Chocolate Mini Morsels, *divided*

Filling
- 2 packages (8 ounces *each*) cream cheese, softened
- ½ cup granulated sugar
- 1 tablespoon vanilla extract
- 2 large eggs
- 2 tablespoons all-purpose flour
- ¾ cup NESTLÉ® CARNATION® Evaporated Milk
- ½ cup sour cream

For Crust

PREHEAT oven to 300°F.

COMBINE cookie crumbs with butter in medium bowl until moistened; press onto bottom of ungreased 9-inch springform pan. Sprinkle with *1 cup* morsels.

For Filling

BEAT cream cheese, sugar and vanilla extract in large mixer bowl until smooth. Beat in eggs and flour. Gradually beat in evaporated milk and sour cream. Pour over crust. Sprinkle with *remaining* morsels.

BAKE for 25 minutes. Cover loosely with foil.

BAKE for additional 30 to 40 minutes or until edge is set but center still moves slightly. Place in refrigerator immediately; refrigerate for 2 hours or until firm. Remove side of springform pan.

Makes 12 to 14 servings

Note: Cheesecake may be baked in 13×9-inch pan. Prepare as above. Bake in preheated 300°F. oven for 20 minutes. Cover loosely with foil. Bake for additional 20 to 30 minutes.

Premier White Buttercream Frosting

8 ounces NESTLÉ® TOLL HOUSE® Premier White Baking Bar, broken into small pieces

⅓ cup heavy whipping cream

1 cup (2 sticks) butter, cut into pieces

1 cup powdered sugar

MICROWAVE baking bars and cream in medium, uncovered, microwave-safe bowl on MEDIUM-HIGH (70%) power for 1 minute; STIR. The bars may retain some of their shape. If necessary, microwave at additional 10- to 15-second intervals, stirring just until melted.

TRANSFER mixture to large mixer bowl; cool to room temperature. Beat in butter until creamy. Gradually beat in powdered sugar until light and fluffy.

Makes 3 cups

Molten Chocolate Cakes

2 tablespoons plus ¾ cup (1½ sticks) butter, *divided*

2 bars (8 ounces) NESTLÉ® TOLL HOUSE® Dark Chocolate Baking Bar, broken into pieces

3 large eggs

3 large egg yolks

¼ cup *plus* 1 tablespoon granulated sugar

1 teaspoon vanilla extract

1 tablespoon all-purpose flour

Powdered sugar

PREHEAT oven to 425°F. Generously butter six (6-ounce) ramekins or custard cups with *2 tablespoons* butter.

STIR *¾ cup* butter and chocolate in medium, *heavy-duty* saucepan over low heat until chocolate is melted and mixture is smooth. Remove from heat. Beat eggs, egg yolks, granulated sugar and vanilla extract in large mixer bowl until thick and pale yellow, about 8 minutes. Fold ⅓ of chocolate mixture into egg mixture. Fold in *remaining* chocolate mixture and flour until well blended. Divide batter evenly among prepared ramekins. Place on baking sheet.

BAKE for 12 to 13 minutes or until sides are set and 1-inch centers move slightly when shaken. Remove from oven to wire rack.

Makes 6 servings

To Serve: Run a thin knife around top edge of cakes to loosen slightly; carefully invert onto serving plates. Lift ramekins off of cakes. Sprinkle with powdered sugar. Serve immediately.

Chunky Pecan Pie Bars

Crust

1½ cups all-purpose flour

½ cup (1 stick) butter or margarine, softened

¼ cup packed brown sugar

Filling

3 large eggs

¾ cup corn syrup

¾ cup granulated sugar

2 tablespoons butter or margarine, melted

1 teaspoon vanilla extract

1¾ cups (11.5-ounce package) NESTLÉ® TOLL HOUSE® Semi-Sweet Chocolate Chunks

1½ cups coarsely chopped pecans

PREHEAT oven to 350°F. Grease 13×9-inch baking pan.

For Crust

BEAT flour, butter and brown sugar in small mixer bowl until crumbly. Press into prepared baking pan.

BAKE for 12 to 15 minutes or until lightly browned.

For Filling

BEAT eggs, corn syrup, granulated sugar, butter and vanilla extract in medium bowl with wire whisk. Stir in chunks and nuts. Pour evenly over baked crust.

BAKE for 25 to 30 minutes or until set. Cool completely in pan on wire rack. Cut into bars.

Makes 3 dozen bars

Seasonal Favorites

Holiday Peppermint Bark

2 cups (12-ounce package) NESTLÉ® TOLL HOUSE® Premier White Morsels

24 hard peppermint candies, unwrapped

LINE baking sheet with wax paper.

MICROWAVE morsels in medium, uncovered, microwave-safe bowl on MEDIUM-HIGH (70%) power for 1 minute; STIR. Morsels may retain some of their original shape. If necessary, microwave at additional 10- to 15-second intervals, stirring just until morsels are melted.

PLACE peppermint candies in *heavy-duty* plastic bag. Crush candies using rolling pin or other heavy object. While holding strainer over melted morsels, pour crushed candy into strainer. Shake to release all small candy pieces; reserve larger candy pieces. Stir morsel-peppermint mixture.

SPREAD mixture to desired thickness on prepared baking sheet. Sprinkle with *reserved* candy pieces; press in lightly. Let stand for about 1 hour or until firm. Break into pieces. Store in airtight container at room temperature.

Makes about 1 pound candy

LIBBY'S® Pumpkin Roll

Cake

- ¼ cup powdered sugar (to sprinkle on towel)
- ¾ cup all-purpose flour
- ½ teaspoon baking powder
- ½ teaspoon baking soda
- ½ teaspoon ground cinnamon
- ½ teaspoon ground cloves
- ¼ teaspoon salt
- 3 large eggs
- 1 cup granulated sugar
- ⅔ cup LIBBY'S® 100% Pure Pumpkin
- 1 cup chopped walnuts (optional)

Filling

- 1 package (8 ounces) cream cheese, at room temperature
- 1 cup powdered sugar, sifted
- 6 tablespoons butter or margarine, softened
- 1 teaspoon vanilla extract

  Powdered sugar (optional)

For Cake

PREHEAT oven to 375°F. Grease 15×10-inch jelly-roll pan; line with wax paper. Grease and flour paper. Sprinkle a thin, cotton kitchen towel with powdered sugar.

COMBINE flour, baking powder, baking soda, cinnamon, cloves and salt in small bowl. Beat eggs and granulated sugar in large mixer bowl until thick. Beat in pumpkin. Stir in flour mixture. Spread evenly into prepared pan. Sprinkle with nuts.

BAKE for 13 to 15 minutes or until top of cake springs back when touched. (If using a dark-colored pan, begin checking for doneness at 11 minutes.) Immediately loosen and turn cake onto prepared towel. Carefully peel off paper. Roll up cake and towel together, starting with narrow end. Cool on wire rack.

For Filling

BEAT cream cheese, powdered sugar, butter and vanilla extract in small mixer bowl until smooth. Carefully unroll cake. Spread cream cheese mixture over cake. Reroll cake. Wrap in plastic wrap and refrigerate at least one hour. Sprinkle with powdered sugar before serving, if desired.

Makes 10 servings

Cranberry Bliss Bars

1 package (16.5 ounces) NESTLÉ® TOLL HOUSE® Refrigerated Sugar Cookie Bar Dough, *divided*

1 cup (8-ounce can) whole-berry cranberry sauce

1 tablespoon cornstarch

½ cup NESTLÉ® TOLL HOUSE® Premier White Morsels, *divided*

4 ounces cream cheese, at room temperature

2 tablespoons butter, softened

¾ cup powdered sugar

½ cup sweetened dried cranberries, chopped

PREHEAT oven to 350°F. Grease 8-inch-square baking pan.

PRESS ¾ *package* (18 squares) cookie dough into prepared baking pan. Refrigerate remaining ¼ *package* (6 squares) cookie dough.

BAKE for 12 minutes; remove from oven to wire rack.

COMBINE cranberry sauce and cornstarch in small bowl; spread over base. Top with teaspoonfuls of *remaining* cookie dough and morsels; press down gently.

BAKE for an additional 20 to 22 minutes or until edges are brown and top is set. Cool completely in pan on wire rack.

BEAT cream cheese, butter and powdered sugar in small mixer bowl until smooth. Spread over cooled base. Sprinkle with cranberries. Refrigerate 1 hour. Cut into 16 bars. Store in covered container in refrigerator

Makes 16 servings

Mini Chip Snowball Cookies

1½ cups (3 sticks) butter or margarine, softened

¾ cup powdered sugar

1 tablespoon vanilla extract

½ teaspoon salt

3 cups all-purpose flour

2 cups (12-ounce package) NESTLÉ® TOLL HOUSE® Semi-Sweet Chocolate Mini Morsels

½ cup finely chopped nuts

Powdered sugar

PREHEAT oven to 375°F.

BEAT butter, sugar, vanilla extract and salt in large mixer bowl until creamy. Gradually beat in flour; stir in morsels and nuts. Shape level tablespoons of dough into 1¼-inch balls. Place on ungreased baking sheets.

BAKE for 10 to 12 minutes or until cookies are set and lightly browned. Remove from oven. Sift powdered sugar over hot cookies on baking sheets. Cool on baking sheets for 10 minutes; remove to wire racks to cool completely. Sprinkle with additional powdered sugar, if desired. Store in airtight containers.

Makes about 5 dozen cookies

NESTLÉ® TOLL HOUSE® Hot Cocoa

½ cup granulated sugar

⅓ cup NESTLÉ® TOLL HOUSE® Baking Cocoa

4 cups milk, *divided*

1 teaspoon vanilla extract

Whipped cream or miniature marshmallows (optional)

COMBINE sugar and cocoa in medium saucepan; stir. Gradually stir in *⅓ cup* milk to make a smooth paste; stir in *remaining* milk.

WARM over medium heat, stirring constantly, until hot (do not boil). Remove from heat; stir in vanilla extract. Top with whipped cream or marshmallows, if desired, before serving.

Makes 4 servings

100-Calorie Pumpkin Pie Tartlets

16 (2½-inch) foil baking cups
  Nonstick cooking spray
¾ cup granulated sugar
 1 tablespoon cornstarch
 1 teaspoon ground cinnamon
 ½ teaspoon ground ginger
 ½ teaspoon salt
 2 large egg whites
 1 can (15 ounces) LIBBY'S®
  100% Pure Pumpkin
 1 can (12 fluid ounces) NESTLÉ®
  CARNATION® Evaporated
  Fat Free Milk
 1 cup fat-free whipped topping
12 small gingersnap cookies,
  broken into ¼-inch pieces

PREHEAT oven to 350°F. Place baking cups on baking sheet with sides. Spray each cup with cooking spray.

COMBINE sugar, cornstarch, cinnamon, ginger and salt in small bowl. Beat egg whites in large bowl. Stir in pumpkin and sugar mixture. Gradually stir in evaporated milk. Spoon ¼ to ⅓ *cup* of mixture into each prepared cup.

BAKE for 25 to 28 minutes or until knife inserted near centers comes out clean. Cool on baking sheet for 20 minutes. Refrigerate for at least 1 hour. Top each with whipped topping and gingersnap crumbs.

Makes 16 servings

Holiday Bread Pudding

16 slices bread, cubed
1 cup dried cranberries or raisins
2 cans (12 fluid ounces *each*) NESTLÉ® CARNATION® Evaporated Milk
4 large eggs, lightly beaten
4 tablespoons butter, melted
¾ cup packed brown sugar
1 tablespoon vanilla extract
1 teaspoon ground cinnamon
½ teaspoon ground nutmeg
Caramel sauce (optional)

PREHEAT oven to 350°F. Grease 12×8-inch baking dish.

COMBINE bread and cranberries in large bowl. Combine evaporated milk, eggs, butter, sugar, vanilla extract, cinnamon and nutmeg in medium bowl. Pour egg mixture over bread mixture; combine well. Pour mixture into prepared baking dish. Let stand for 10 minutes.

BAKE for 35 to 45 minutes or until knife inserted in center comes out clean. Top with caramel sauce.

Makes 8 servings

Spiced Pumpkin Bread

2 cups all-purpose flour

5 teaspoons ground allspice or pumpkin pie spice

2 teaspoons baking powder

½ teaspoon baking soda

½ teaspoon salt

1 cup LIBBY'S® 100% Pure Pumpkin

1 cup packed brown sugar

½ cup Apple NESTLÉ® JUICY JUICE® All Natural 100% Juice

2 large eggs

2 tablespoons vegetable oil

1 teaspoon vanilla extract

PREHEAT oven to 350°F.

SIFT flour, allspice, baking powder, baking soda and salt into medium bowl. Combine pumpkin, sugar, Juicy Juice, eggs, oil and vanilla extract in large bowl; stir well. Stir in flour mixture just until moistened. Spoon into greased 9×5-inch loaf pan.

BAKE for 65 to 70 minutes or until wooden pick inserted in center comes out clean. Cool in pan on wire rack for 10 minutes; remove to wire rack to cool completely.

Makes 1 loaf (16 slices per loaf)

Chocolaty Cherry Biscotti

2 cups (12-ounce package)
  NESTLÉ® TOLL HOUSE®
  Semi-Sweet Chocolate
  Morsels, *divided*

2 cups all-purpose flour

¼ cup NESTLÉ® TOLL HOUSE®
  Baking Cocoa

1 teaspoon baking powder

½ teaspoon salt

¾ cup packed brown sugar

¼ cup (½ stick) butter, softened

2 large eggs

½ teaspoon vanilla extract

1 cup (about 5 ounces) dried
  cherries, chopped

PREHEAT oven to 325°F. Grease baking sheet.

MICROWAVE ⅔ cup morsels in small, uncovered, microwave-safe bowl on HIGH (100%) power for 45 seconds; STIR. The morsels may retain some of their original shape. If necessary, microwave at additional 10- to 15-second intervals, stirring just until morsels are melted.

COMBINE flour, cocoa, baking powder and salt in small bowl. Beat sugar and butter in large bowl until light and fluffy. Add eggs and vanilla extract; beat until combined. Stir in melted chocolate. Gradually stir in flour mixture. Stir in cherries and *1 cup* morsels.

SHAPE dough with floured hands on prepared baking sheet into two 9×2½-inch logs.

BAKE for 40 minutes or until slightly firm to the touch and cracked on top. Cool on baking sheet for 10 minutes. Slide log onto cutting board and cut each log into 12, ¾-inch slices. Return to baking sheet cut side down. Bake, turning once, for 20 minutes or until firm. Remove to wire rack to cool completely.

PLACE *remaining ⅓ cup* morsels in small, heavy-duty plastic bag. Microwave on HIGH (100%) power for 30 to 45 seconds; knead. Cut a tiny corner from bag and drizzle over cooled biscotti. Let stand until drizzle is set. Store in tightly covered container at room temperature.

Makes 2 dozen biscotti

Tip: NESTLÉ® TOLL HOUSE® Semi-Sweet Chocolate Mini Morsels can be substituted for the Semi-Sweet Chocolate Morsels.

Chocolate Gingerbread Boys and Girls

2 cups (12-ounce package) NESTLÉ® TOLL HOUSE® Semi-Sweet Chocolate Morsels, *divided*

2¾ cups all-purpose flour

1 teaspoon baking soda

½ teaspoon salt

½ teaspoon ground ginger

½ teaspoon ground cinnamon

3 tablespoons butter or margarine, softened

3 tablespoons granulated sugar

½ cup molasses

¼ cup water

1 container (16 ounces) prepared vanilla frosting, colored as desired, or colored icing in tubes

MICROWAVE *1½ cups* morsels in medium, uncovered, microwave-safe bowl on HIGH (100%) power for 1 minute; STIR. The morsels may retain some of their original shape. If necessary, microwave at additional 10- to 15-second intervals, stirring just until melted. Cool to room temperature.

COMBINE flour, baking soda, salt, ginger and cinnamon in medium bowl. Beat butter and sugar in small mixer bowl until creamy; beat in molasses and melted chocolate. Gradually add flour mixture alternately with water, beating until smooth. Cover; refrigerate for 1 hour or until firm.

PREHEAT oven to 350°F.

ROLL *half* of dough to ¼-inch thickness on floured surface with floured rolling pin. Cut dough into gingerbread boy and girl shapes using cookie cutters or a stencil. Place on ungreased baking sheets. Repeat with remaining dough.

BAKE for 5 to 6 minutes or until edges are set but centers are still slightly soft. Cool on baking sheets for 2 minutes; remove to wire racks to cool completely.

PLACE *remaining* morsels in *heavy-duty* plastic bag. Microwave on HIGH (100%) power for 30 to 45 seconds; knead. Microwave for 10 seconds; knead until smooth. Cut tiny corner from bag; squeeze to pipe chocolate. Decorate cookies with piped chocolate and prepared frosting or icing.

Makes about 2½ dozen cookies

LIBBY'S® Pumpkin Cranberry Bread

3 cups all-purpose flour

1 tablespoon plus 2 teaspoons pumpkin pie spice

2 teaspoons baking soda

1½ teaspoons salt

3 cups granulated sugar

1 can (15 ounces) LIBBY'S® 100% Pure Pumpkin

4 large eggs

1 cup vegetable oil

½ cup orange juice or water

1 cup sweetened dried, fresh or frozen cranberries

PREHEAT oven to 350°F. Grease and flour two 9×5-inch loaf pans.

COMBINE flour, pumpkin pie spice, baking soda and salt in large bowl. Combine sugar, pumpkin, eggs, oil and juice in large mixer bowl; beat until just blended. Add pumpkin mixture to flour mixture; stir just until moistened. Fold in cranberries. Spoon batter into prepared loaf pans.

BAKE for 60 to 65 minutes or until wooden pick inserted in center comes out clean. Cool in pans on wire racks for 10 minutes; remove to wire racks to cool completely.

Makes 2 loaves (12 slices per loaf)

For three 8×4-inch loaf pans:
Prepare as directed above. Bake for 55 to 60 minutes.

For five or six 5×3-inch mini-loaf pans: Prepare as directed above. Bake for 50 to 55 minutes.

Pumpkin Cheesecake

Crust
- 1½ cups graham cracker crumbs
- ⅓ cup butter or margarine, melted
- ¼ granulated sugar

Cheesecake
- 3 packages (8 ounces *each*) cream cheese, softened
- 1 cup granulated sugar
- ¼ cup packed light brown sugar
- 2 large eggs
- 1 can (15 ounces) LIBBY'S® 100% Pure Pumpkin
- ⅔ cup (5 fluid-ounce can) NESTLÉ® CARNATION® Evaporated Milk
- 2 tablespoons cornstarch
- 1¼ teaspoons ground cinnamon
- ½ teaspoon ground nutmeg

Topping
- 1 container (16 ounces) sour cream, at room temperature
- ⅓ cup granulated sugar
- 1 teaspoon vanilla extract

PREHEAT oven to 350°F.

For Crust

COMBINE graham cracker crumbs, butter and granulated sugar in medium bowl. Press onto bottom and 1 inch up side of 9-inch springform pan. Bake for 6 to 8 minutes (do not allow to brown). Cool on wire rack for 10 minutes.

For Cheesecake

BEAT cream cheese, granulated sugar and brown sugar in large mixer bowl until fluffy. Beat in eggs, pumpkin and evaporated milk. Add cornstarch, cinnamon and nutmeg; beat well. Pour Into crust.

BAKE for 55 to 60 minutes or until edge is set but center still moves slightly.

For Topping

COMBINE sour cream, granulated sugar and vanilla extract in small bowl; mix well. Spread over surface of warm cheesecake. Bake for 5 minutes. Cool on wire rack. Refrigerate for several hours or overnight. Remove side of springform pan.

Makes 16 servings

Double Layer Pumpkin Pie

4 ounces cream cheese, softened

1 tablespoon NESTLÉ® CARNATION® Evaporated Milk, chilled

1 tablespoon granulated sugar

1 *prepared* 8-inch (6-ounce) graham cracker pie crust

1½ cups frozen whipped topping, thawed

1 cup NESTLÉ® CARNATION® Evaporated Milk, chilled

2 packages (3.4 ounces *each*) vanilla instant pudding and pie filling mix

1 can (15 ounces) LIBBY'S® 100% Pure Pumpkin

2 teaspoons pumpkin pie spice*

Whipped topping (optional)

Note: 1 teaspoon ground cinnamon, ½ teaspoon ground ginger and ¼ teaspoon ground cloves can be substituted for pumpkin pie spice.

COMBINE cream cheese, 1 tablespoon evaporated milk and sugar in large bowl with wire whisk until smooth. Gently stir in whipped topping. Spread on bottom of pie crust.

POUR 1 cup evaporated milk into bowl. Add pudding mixes. Beat with wire whisk for 1 minute (mixture will be thick). Stir in pumpkin and pumpkin pie spice with wire whisk until well mixed. Spread over cream cheese layer.

REFRIGERATE for 4 hours or until set. Garnish with additional whipped topping, if desired.

Makes 8 servings

Rich & Chocolatey

NESTLÉ® Very Best Fudge

3 cups granulated sugar

1 can (12 fluid ounces) NESTLÉ® CARNATION® Evaporated Milk

¼ cup (½ stick) butter or margarine

½ teaspoon salt

4 cups miniature marshmallows

4 cups (24 ounces) or two 12-ounce packages NESTLÉ® TOLL HOUSE® Semi-Sweet Chocolate Morsels

1 cup chopped pecans or walnuts (optional)

2 teaspoons vanilla extract

LINE 13×9-inch baking pan or two 8-inch-square baking pans with foil.

COMBINE sugar, evaporated milk, butter and salt in 4- to 5-quart *heavy-duty* saucepan. Bring to a *full rolling boil* over medium heat, stirring constantly. Boil, stirring constantly, for 4 to 5 minutes. Remove from heat.

STIR in marshmallows, morsels, nuts and vanilla extract. Stir vigorously for 1 minute or until marshmallows are melted. Pour into prepared pan(s). Refrigerate for 2 hours or until firm.

Lift from pan; remove foil. Cut into pieces. Store tightly covered in refrigerator. Makes about 4 pounds.

FOR MILK CHOCOLATE FUDGE:

SUBSTITUTE 3½ cups (23 ounces) or 2 packages (11.5 ounces each) NESTLÉ® TOLL HOUSE® Milk Chocolate Morsels for Semi-Sweet Chocolate Morsels.

FOR BUTTERSCOTCH FUDGE:

SUBSTITUTE 3⅓ cups (22 ounces) or 2 packages (11 ounces each) NESTLÉ® TOLL HOUSE® Butterscotch Flavored Morsels for Semi-Sweet Chocolate Morsels.

FOR PEANUTTY CHOCOLATE FUDGE:

SUBSTITUTE 3⅓ cups (22 ounces) or 2 packages (11 ounces each) NESTLÉ® TOLL HOUSE® Peanut Butter & Milk Chocolate Morsels for Semi-Sweet Chocolate Morsels and ½ cup chopped peanuts for pecans or walnuts.

Makes 48 servings (2 pieces per serving)

Toasted Almond Truffles

½ cup **NESTLÉ® CARNATION® Evaporated Milk**

¼ cup **granulated sugar**

1¾ cups (11.5-ounce package) **NESTLÉ® TOLL HOUSE® Milk Chocolate Morsels**

½ to 1 teaspoon **almond or vanilla extract**

1 cup **sliced almonds, toasted, finely chopped**

COMBINE evaporated milk and sugar in small, *heavy-duty* saucepan. Bring to a *full rolling boil* over medium-low heat, stirring constantly. Boil, stirring constantly, for 3 minutes. Remove from heat.

STIR in morsels. Stir vigorously until mixture is smooth. Stir in almond extract. Refrigerate for 1½ to 2 hours. Shape into 1-inch balls; roll in nuts. Cover; refrigerate until ready to serve.

Makes 2 dozen truffles

Chocolate Velvet Pie

1¾ cups (11.5-ounce package)
  NESTLÉ® TOLL HOUSE® Milk
  Chocolate Morsels

1 package (8 ounces) cream
  cheese, softened

1 teaspoon vanilla extract

1 cup heavy whipping cream,
  whipped

1 *prepared* 8-inch (6-ounce)
  chocolate crumb crust

  Sweetened whipped cream
  (optional)

2 ounces NESTLÉ® TOLL HOUSE®
  Semi-Sweet Chocolate
  Baking Bar, made into curls

  Chopped nuts (optional)

MICROWAVE morsels in medium, uncovered, microwave-safe bowl on MEDIUM-HIGH (70%) power for 1 minute; STIR. The morsels may retain some of their original shape. If necessary, microwave at additional 10- to 15-second intervals, stirring just until melted. Cool to room temperature.

BEAT melted chocolate, cream cheese and vanilla extract in large mixer bowl until light in color. Fold in whipped cream. Spoon into crust. Refrigerate for at least 2 hours or until firm. Top with sweetened whipped cream, chocolate curls and nuts.

Makes 8 servings

Chocolate Peanut Butter Tart

Crust
- 1½ **cups all-purpose flour**
- ¼ **cup** *plus* **1 tablespoon finely chopped peanuts**
- ¼ **cup granulated sugar**
- 10 **tablespoons butter, melted**
- **Nonstick cooking spray**

Filling
- 1¼ **cups heavy whipping cream**
- 2 **cups (12-ounce package) NESTLE® TOLL HOUSE® Semi-Sweet Chocolate Morsels**
- 2 **tablespoons butter, softened**
- 1 **cup creamy peanut butter**
- 2 **tablespoons powdered sugar**

For Crust:

PREHEAT oven to 400°F.

COMBINE flour, ¼ *cup* peanuts, granulated sugar and butter in medium bowl. Press dough evenly onto bottom and side of ungreased 9- to 10-inch tart pan with removable bottom. Spray 10-inch piece of aluminum foil with nonstick cooking spray. Gently press oiled side down on top of dough. Using a fork, poke holes through foil and crust to create air vents.

BAKE for 15 minutes; remove foil. Continue baking for an additional 5 to 10 minutes or until edges are golden brown and bottom of crust is baked. Cool completely in pan on wire rack.

For Filling:

HEAT cream in medium, *heavy-duty* saucepan over low heat, stirring occasionally until it just comes to a boil. Remove from heat. Stir in morsels and butter. Let stand for 3 minutes. Stir until mixture is smooth. Refrigerate for 20 minutes.

COMBINE peanut butter and powdered sugar in small bowl.

To Assemble:

SPOON peanut butter filling onto bottom of prepared crust and spread evenly. Pour ganache on top. Gently tap the pan on the counter to create a smooth surface. Sprinkle surface with remaining tablespoon of chopped peanuts. Refrigerate for 3 hours or until firm. Cut into slices and serve.

Makes 12 servings

Milk Chocolate Almond Brickle

1¼ cups almonds, toasted and
    coarsely chopped

1 cup (2 sticks) butter

1½ cups packed brown sugar

1¾ cups (11.5-ounce package)
    NESTLÉ® TOLL HOUSE® Milk
    Chocolate Morsels

SPRINKLE nuts over bottom of well-greased 13×9-inch baking pan.

MELT butter in medium, *heavy-duty* saucepan over medium heat. Stir in sugar. Bring to a boil, stirring constantly. Boil, stirring constantly, for 7 minutes. Pour hot mixture over nuts; let stand for 5 minutes. Sprinkle with morsels. Let stand for 5 minutes or until morsels are shiny and soft; spread evenly.

REFRIGERATE for about 20 minutes. Break into bite-size pieces.

Makes about 50 pieces

Chocolate Caramels

1 cup (2 sticks) butter

1 cup granulated sugar

1 cup packed dark brown sugar

1 cup light corn syrup

1 can (14 ounces) NESTLÉ® CARNATION® Sweetened Condensed Milk

2 packets (1 ounce *each*) NESTLÉ® TOLL HOUSE® CHOCO BAKE® Pre-Melted Unsweetened Chocolate Flavor

1 teaspoon vanilla extract

LINE 8-inch-square baking pan with foil; grease.

COMBINE butter, granulated sugar, brown sugar and corn syrup in medium, *heavy-duty* saucepan. Cook over medium heat, stirring constantly, until mixture comes to a boil and butter is melted. Add sweetened condensed milk and Choco Bake. Cook over medium-low heat, stirring frequently, for 25 to 35 minutes or until mixture reaches 245°F on candy thermometer. Remove from heat; stir in vanilla extract. Immediately pour into prepared pan. Cool at room temperature.

LIFT from pan; remove foil. Cut into about ½-inch squares or size desired and wrap individually in plastic wrap, twisting ends. Store in refrigerator or at room temperature; use within 7 to 10 days.

Makes 36 servings
(2 pieces per serving)

Chocolate Mudslide Frozen Pie

1 cup (6 ounces) NESTLÉ®
    TOLL HOUSE® Semi-Sweet
    Chocolate Morsels

1 teaspoon NESCAFÉ TASTER'S
    CHOICE House Blend
    100% Pure Instant Coffee
    Granules

1 teaspoon hot water

¾ cup sour cream

½ cup granulated sugar

1 teaspoon vanilla extract

1 *prepared* 9-inch (6 ounces)
    chocolate crumb crust

1½ cups heavy whipping cream

1 cup powdered sugar

¼ cup NESTLÉ® TOLL HOUSE®
    Baking Cocoa

2 tablespoons NESTLÉ® TOLL
    HOUSE® Semi-Sweet
    Chocolate Mini Morsels

MELT 1 cup morsels in small, *heavy-duty* saucepan over lowest possible heat. When morsels begin to melt, remove from heat; stir. Return to heat for a few seconds at a time, stirring until smooth. Remove from heat; cool for 10 minutes.

COMBINE coffee granules and water in medium bowl. Add sour cream, granulated sugar and vanilla extract; stir until granulated sugar is dissolved. Stir in melted chocolate until smooth. Spread into crust; refrigerate.

BEAT cream, powdered sugar and cocoa in small mixer bowl until stiff peaks form. Spread or pipe over chocolate layer. Sprinkle with mini morsels. Freeze for at least 6 hours or until firm.

Makes 8 servings

Chocolate Mint Truffles

1¾ cups (11.5-ounce package)
    NESTLÉ® TOLL HOUSE® Milk
    Chocolate Morsels

1 cup (6 ounces) NESTLÉ®
    TOLL HOUSE® Semi-Sweet
    Chocolate Morsels

¾ cup heavy whipping cream

1 tablespoon peppermint
    extract

1½ cups finely chopped walnuts,
    toasted, or NESTLÉ® TOLL
    HOUSE® Baking Cocoa

LINE baking sheet with wax paper.

PLACE milk chocolate and semi-sweet morsels in large mixer bowl. Heat cream to a gentle boil in small saucepan; pour over morsels. Let stand for 1 minute; stir until smooth. Stir in peppermint extract. Cover with plastic wrap; refrigerate for 35 to 45 minutes or until slightly thickened. Stir just until color lightens slightly. (*Do not* overmix or truffles will be grainy.)

DROP by rounded teaspoonfuls onto prepared baking sheet; refrigerate for 10 to 15 minutes. Shape into balls; roll in walnuts or cocoa. Store in airtight container in refrigerator.

Makes about 48 truffles

Variation: After rolling chocolate mixture into balls, freeze for 30 to 40 minutes. Microwave 1¾ cups (11.5-ounce package) NESTLÉ® TOLL HOUSE® Milk Chocolate Morsels and 3 tablespoons vegetable shortening in medium, uncovered, microwave-safe bowl on MEDIUM-HIGH (70%) power for 1 minute; STIR. Morsels may retain some of their original shape. If necessary, microwave at additional 10- to 15-second intervals, stirring just until melted. Dip truffles into chocolate mixture; shake off excess. Place on foil-lined baking sheets. Refrigerate for 15 to 20 minutes or until set. Store in airtight container in refrigerator.

Chocolate Indulgence Holiday Gifting Sauce

2 cups (12-ounce package) NESTLÉ® TOLL HOUSE® Semi-Sweet Chocolate Morsels

1 cup heavy whipping cream

2 tablespoons light corn syrup

2 to 3 tablespoons flavored liqueur or ½ teaspoon flavored extract (optional)

COMBINE morsels, cream and corn syrup in large microwave-safe bowl.

MICROWAVE uncovered, on HIGH (100%) power for 1 minute; STIR. If necessary, microwave at additional 20- to 30-second intervals, stirring until morsels are melted and sauce is smooth. Add liqueur or extract; mix well.

SERVE warm as a dipping sauce for fresh fruit or spoon over ice cream or cake. Store remaining sauce tightly covered in refrigerator. Makes about 2 cups.

FOR GIFTING:

TRANSFER sauce to clean gifting jars; seal well. Refrigerate up to 7 days.

NOTE: 1¾ cups (11.5-ounce package) NESTLÉ® TOLL HOUSE® Milk Chocolate Morsels can be substituted for the Semi-Sweet Chocolate Morsels.

Makes 16 servings, 2 tablespoons each

Delicious Dilemma

1 package (16.5 ounces) NESTLÉ® TOLL HOUSE® Refrigerated Sugar Cookie Bar Dough

½ cup seedless red raspberry jam

1 cup (6 ounces) NESTLÉ® TOLL HOUSE® Premier White Morsels, *divided*

1 cup (6 ounces) NESTLÉ® TOLL HOUSE® Semi-Sweet Chocolate Mini Morsels, *divided*

1 package (8 ounces) cream cheese, softened

¼ cup granulated sugar

1 large egg

1 teaspoon vanilla extract

1 cup slivered almonds

PREHEAT oven to 325°F. Grease 13×9-inch baking pan.

PLACE bar in prepared baking pan. Allow to soften for 5 to 10 minutes. Using fingertips, pat dough gently to cover bottom and one inch up side of pan.

STIR raspberry jam in small bowl until smooth. Spread the jam evenly over the dough leaving a ½-inch border. Sprinkle ⅔ cup white morsels and ⅔ cup mini morsels over the jam.

BEAT cream cheese and sugar in medium mixer bowl until smooth. Add egg and vanilla extract; beat until combined. Spread cream cheese mixture over the morsels. Sprinkle the top with *remaining* ⅓ cup morsels and almonds.

BAKE for 35 to 40 minutes or until sides are golden brown and center is set. Cool completely in pan on wire rack. Refrigerate for at least 2 hours. Cut into bars.

Makes 2 dozen bars

Spread Joy

Chunky Chocolate Chip Peanut Butter Cookies

1¼ cups all-purpose flour

½ teaspoon baking soda

½ teaspoon ground cinnamon

½ teaspoon salt

¾ cup (1½ sticks) butter or margarine, softened

½ cup packed brown sugar

½ cup granulated sugar

½ cup creamy peanut butter

1 large egg

1 teaspoon vanilla extract

2 cups (12-ounce package) NESTLÉ® TOLL HOUSE® Semi-Sweet Chocolate Morsels

½ cup coarsely chopped peanuts

PREHEAT oven to 375°F.

COMBINE flour, baking soda, cinnamon and salt in small bowl. Beat butter, brown sugar, granulated sugar and peanut butter in large mixer bowl until creamy. Beat in egg and vanilla extract. Gradually beat in flour mixture. Stir in morsels and peanuts.

DROP dough by rounded tablespoons onto ungreased baking sheets. Press down slightly to flatten into 2-inch circles.

BAKE for 7 to 10 minutes or until edges are set but centers are still soft. Cool on baking sheets for 4 minutes; remove to wire racks to cool completely.

Makes about 3 dozen cookies

Very Merry Cookie Wreath

1 package (16.5 ounces) NESTLÉ TOLL HOUSE Refrigerated Mini Chocolate Chip Cookie Bar Dough

1 container (16 ounces) prepared vanilla frosting

Green food coloring

14×17-inch piece of cardboard for base, covered in foil or parchment paper or large flat platter

NESTLÉ® TOLL HOUSE® Morsels (such as Semi-Sweet Chocolate, Milk Chocolate, Premier White)

Assorted NESTLÉ® TOLL HOUSE® Holiday Candies (WONKA® Gobstoppers® Snowballs, NERDS® or SPREE®)

Decorator sprinkles, candies and sugars

20-inch strip of strawberry fruit-flavored snack in 3-foot rolls

PREPARE cookies following package directions. Cool on baking sheets for 2 minutes. Remove to wire rack to cool completely.

COMBINE frosting and food coloring in small bowl to shade of green desired.

SPREAD heaping teaspoons of frosting on flat sides of cookies.

ARRANGE 15 cookies on the base or platter in a 12-inch circle to form outer ring of wreath.

ARRANGE 12 cookies inside the outer ring of cookies, forming inside ring of wreath. Adhered cookies can be moved to create more space.

ARRANGE remaining 13 cookies on base ring for a second layer.

DECORATE with remaining frosting, morsels, candies, sprinkles and sugars as desired. Attach bow to top of wreath.

TO MAKE BOW:

CUT four 5-inch strips from fruit snack roll. Peel off paper backing. Cut a small "V" on end of two strips. Form loops with remaining two strips; pinch ends together. Place loops on top of strips. Pinch all together to make bow!

Tips:

- For easier decorating, 1 cup of icing can be spooned into resealable, *heavy-duty* plastic bag; seal. Cut small corner of bag. Squeeze bag to use. Fill with additional icing as needed. Store any leftover icing covered in refrigerator for up to 30 days.

- Cookies can also be made into a tree, initials or any other shape desired.

Zesty Orange Cookie Cups

1 cup (2 sticks) butter, softened

½ cup granulated sugar

2 cups all-purpose flour

2 cups (12-ounce package) NESTLÉ® TOLL HOUSE® Premier White Morsels

2 large eggs

1 can (14 ounces) NESTLÉ® CARNATION® Sweetened Condensed Milk

½ to ¾ teaspoon orange extract

1 tablespoon grated orange peel (1 medium orange)

PREHEAT oven to 350°F. Grease 48 mini-muffin cups.

BEAT butter and sugar in medium mixer bowl until creamy. Add flour; beat until mixture is evenly moist, crumbly and can be formed into balls. Shape dough into 1-inch balls. Press 1 ball onto bottom and up side of each prepared muffin cup to form well. Place *5 morsels* in *each* well.

BEAT eggs in medium bowl with wire whisk. Stir in sweetened condensed milk and orange extract. Spoon almost a measuring tablespoon of mixture into each muffin cup, filling about ¾ full.

BAKE for 15 to 17 minutes or until centers are puffed and edges are just beginning to brown. Upon removing from oven, gently run knife around *each* cup. While still warm, top each cup with 8 to 10 morsels (they will soften and retain their shape). Cool completely in pans on wire racks. With tip of knife, remove cookie cups from muffin pans. Top with grated orange peel just before serving. Store in covered container in refrigerator.

Makes 4 dozen cookie cups

TOLL HOUSE® Party Mix

2 cups toasted cereal squares

2 cups small pretzel twists

1 cup dry-roasted peanuts

1 cup (about 20) caramels, unwrapped and coarsely chopped

1⅔ to 2 cups (11- to 12-ounce package) NESTLÉ® TOLL HOUSE® Semi-Sweet Chocolate, Milk Chocolate, Butterscotch Flavored or Premier White Morsels

COAT 13×9-inch baking pan with nonstick cooking spray.

COMBINE cereal, pretzels, peanuts and caramels in large bowl.

MICROWAVE morsels in medium, uncovered, microwave-safe bowl on MEDIUM-HIGH (70%) power for 1 minute; STIR. Morsels may retain some of their original shape. If necessary, microwave at additional 10- to 15-second intervals, stirring just until morsels are melted. Pour over cereal mixture; stir to coat evenly.

SPREAD mixture in prepared baking pan; cool for 30 to 45 minutes or until firm. Break into bite-size pieces. Store in airtight container.

Makes 8 servings

Spiced Pumpkin Fudge

2 cups granulated sugar

1 cup packed light brown sugar

⅔ cup (5 fluid-ounce can) NESTLÉ® CARNATION® Evaporated Milk

½ cup LIBBY'S® 100% Pure Pumpkin

¾ cup (1½ sticks) butter or margarine

2 teaspoons pumpkin pie spice

2 cups (12-ounce package) NESTLÉ® TOLL HOUSE® Premier White Morsels

1 jar (7 ounces) marshmallow crème

1 cup chopped pecans

1½ teaspoons vanilla extract

LINE 13×9-inch baking pan with foil.

COMBINE granulated sugar, brown sugar, evaporated milk, pumpkin, butter and spice in medium, *heavy-duty* saucepan. Bring to a *full rolling boil* over medium heat, stirring constantly. Boil, stirring constantly, for 10 to 12 minutes or until candy thermometer reaches 234° to 240°F (soft-ball stage).

QUICKLY STIR in morsels, marshmallow crème, nuts and vanilla extract. Stir vigorously for 1 minute or until morsels are melted. Immediately pour into prepared pan. Let stand on wire rack for 2 hours or until completely cooled. Refrigerate tightly covered. To cut, lift from pan; remove foil. Cut into 1-inch pieces.

Makes 4 dozen servings
(2 pieces per serving)

Chocolate-Cherry Thumbprints

2 cups (12-ounce package)
  NESTLÉ® TOLL HOUSE®
  Semi-Sweet Chocolate
  Morsels, *divided*

1¾ cups quick or old-fashioned
  oats

1½ cups all-purpose flour

¼ cup NESTLÉ® TOLL HOUSE®
  Baking Cocoa

1 teaspoon baking powder

¼ teaspoon salt (optional)

¾ cup granulated sugar

⅔ cup butter or margarine,
  softened

2 large eggs

1 teaspoon vanilla extract

2 cups (two 10-ounce jars)
  maraschino cherries,
  drained and patted dry

MICROWAVE *1 cup* morsels in small, uncovered, microwave-safe bowl on HIGH (100%) power for 1 minute; STIR. The morsels may retain some of their original shape. If necessary, microwave at additional 10- to 15-second intervals, stirring just until melted. Combine oats, flour, cocoa, baking powder and salt in medium bowl.

BEAT sugar, butter, eggs and vanilla extract in large mixer bowl until smooth. Beat in melted chocolate. Stir in oat mixture. Cover; refrigerate dough for 1 hour.

PREHEAT oven to 350°F.

SHAPE dough into 1-inch balls; press thumb into tops to make deep depression. Place 2 inches apart on ungreased baking sheet. Fill each depression with maraschino cherry.

BAKE for 10 to 12 minutes or until set. Cool on baking sheets for 2 minutes; remove to wire racks to cool completely. Melt *remaining* morsels; drizzle over cookies.

Makes about 4 dozen cookies

Tropical Sunshine Cake

1 package (18.25 ounces)
   yellow cake mix

1 can (12 fluid ounces) NESTLÉ®
   CARNATION® Evaporated
   Milk

2 large eggs

1 can (20 ounces) crushed
   pineapple in juice, drained
   (juice reserved), *divided*

½ cup chopped almonds

¾ cup sifted powdered sugar

1 cup flaked coconut, toasted

   Whipped cream

PREHEAT oven to 350°F. Grease
13×9-inch baking pan.

COMBINE cake mix, evaporated
milk and eggs in large mixer bowl.
Beat on low speed for 2 minutes. Stir
in *1 cup* pineapple. Pour batter into
prepared baking pan. Sprinkle with
almonds.

BAKE for 30 to 35 minutes or until
wooden pick inserted in center
comes out clean. Cool in pan on wire
rack for 15 minutes.

COMBINE sugar and 2 tablespoons
reserved pineapple juice in small
bowl; mix until smooth. Spread over
warm cake; sprinkle with coconut
and *remaining* pineapple. Cool
completely before serving. Top with
whipped cream, if desired.

Makes 12 servings

Oatmeal-Chip Cookie Mix in a Jar

⅔ cup all-purpose flour

½ teaspoon baking soda

½ teaspoon ground cinnamon

¼ teaspoon salt

⅓ cup packed brown sugar

⅓ cup granulated sugar

¾ cup **NESTLÉ® TOLL HOUSE®** Semi-Sweet Chocolate or Butterscotch Flavored Morsels

1½ cups quick or old-fashioned oats

½ cup chopped nuts

COMBINE flour, baking soda, cinnamon and salt in small bowl. Place flour mixture in 1-quart jar. Layer remaining ingredients in order listed, pressing firmly after each layer. Seal with lid and decorate with fabric and ribbon.

Recipe to Attach

BEAT ½ cup (1 stick) softened butter or margarine, 1 large egg and ½ teaspoon vanilla extract in large mixer bowl until blended. Add cookie mix; mix well, breaking up any clumps. Drop by rounded tablespoon onto ungreased baking sheets. Bake in preheated 375°F oven for 8 to 10 minutes. Cool on baking sheets for 2 minutes; remove to wire racks.

Makes about 2 dozen cookies

Chocolate Chip Shells

2 cups all-purpose flour

1⅓ cups (about 8 ounces)
      NESTLÉ® TOLL HOUSE®
      Semi-Sweet Chocolate
      Morsels, *divided*

4 large eggs

1 cup granulated sugar

1 tablespoon orange liqueur
      (such as Cointreau) or
      1 teaspoon orange extract

1 teaspoon vanilla extract

2 tablespoons (about 1 orange)
      grated orange peel

1 cup (2 sticks) unsalted butter,
      melted

   Sifted powdered sugar

PREHEAT oven to 350°F. Generously grease and flour madeleine baking pan(s).

COMBINE flour and *1 cup* morsels in medium bowl. Beat eggs, granulated sugar, orange liqueur, vanilla extract and orange peel in large mixer bowl until light in color. Fold flour mixture and butter alternately into egg mixture, beginning and ending with flour mixture. Spoon heaping tablespoon of batter into each prepared mold.

BAKE for 10 to 12 minutes or until wooden pick inserted in center comes out clean. Cool in pan(s) for 1 minute. With tip of knife, release onto wire racks to cool completely. Wash, grease and flour pan(s). Repeat with *remaining* batter.

SPRINKLE madeleines very lightly with powdered sugar. Microwave *remaining* morsels in *heavy-duty* plastic bag on HIGH (100%) power for 30 seconds; knead bag to mix. Microwave at additional 10-second intervals, kneading until smooth. Cut a small hole in corner of bag; squeeze to drizzle over madeleines. Allow chocolate to cool and set before serving.

Makes about 2½ dozen madeleines

Chocolate Truffle Tart

Crust
- ⅔ cup all-purpose flour
- ½ cup powdered sugar
- ½ cup ground walnuts
- 6 tablespoons butter or margarine, softened
- ⅓ cup NESTLÉ® TOLL HOUSE® Baking Cocoa

Filling
- 1¼ cups heavy whipping cream
- ¼ cup granulated sugar
- 2 cups (12-ounce package) NESTLÉ® TOLL HOUSE® Semi-Sweet Chocolate Morsels
- 2 tablespoons seedless raspberry jam
- Sweetened whipped cream (optional)
- Fresh raspberries (optional)

For Crust

PREHEAT oven to 350°F.

BEAT flour, powdered sugar, nuts, butter and cocoa in large mixer bowl until soft dough forms. Press dough onto bottom and up side of ungreased 9- or 9½-inch fluted tart pan with removable bottom or 9-inch pie plate.

BAKE for 12 to 14 minutes or until puffed. Cool completely in pan on wire rack.

For Filling

BRING cream and granulated sugar in medium saucepan *just to a boil,* stirring occasionally. Remove from heat. Stir in morsels and jam; let stand for 5 minutes. Whisk until smooth. Transfer to small mixer bowl. Cover; refrigerate for 45 to 60 minutes or until mixture is cooled and slightly thickened.

BEAT for 20 to 30 seconds or just until color lightens slightly. Spoon into crust. Refrigerate until firm. Remove side of pan; garnish with whipped cream and raspberries.

Makes 12 servings

Savory & Satisfying

Italian-Style Mac & Cheese with Chicken Sausage

2 cups (8 ounces) dry elbow macaroni (regular or whole wheat)

1 can (12 fluid ounces) NESTLÉ® CARNATION® Evaporated Lowfat 2% Milk

2 cups (8-ounce package) shredded Italian-style 4- or 5-cheese blend

2 links (6 ounces) fully-cooked Italian-seasoned chicken sausage, cut into ¼-inch slices

½ teaspoon garlic powder

½ teaspoon ground black pepper

1 cup cherry tomatoes, cut in half

2 tablespoons finely sliced fresh basil leaves

PREPARE pasta according to package directions; drain.

MEANWHILE, COMBINE evaporated milk, cheese, sausage, garlic powder and black pepper in medium saucepan. Cook over medium-low heat, stirring occasionally, until cheese is melted. Remove from heat.

ADD pasta to cheese sauce; stir until combined. Add tomatoes and basil; stir gently until mixed in.

Makes 6 servings (1 cup each)

Tip: Different flavors of chicken sausage can be substituted.

Scalloped Potatoes

2 pounds (about 6 medium) potatoes, peeled and thinly sliced

3 tablespoons butter or margarine

¼ cup chopped onion

3 tablespoons all-purpose flour

1 teaspoon salt

¼ teaspoon ground black pepper

1 can (12 fluid ounces) NESTLÉ® CARNATION® Evaporated Milk

1 cup water

⅓ cup grated Parmesan cheese

PREHEAT oven to 350°F. Grease 11×7-inch baking dish.

PLACE potatoes in large saucepan. Cover with water; bring to a boil. Cook over medium-high heat for 3 to 4 minutes; drain. Set aside.

HEAT butter in same saucepan over medium heat. Add onion; cook, stirring occasionally, for 1 to 2 minutes or until onion is tender. Stir in flour, salt and pepper. Gradually stir in evaporated milk and water. Cook, stirring constantly, until mixture comes to a boil. Remove from heat. Arrange potatoes in prepared baking dish; pour milk mixture over potatoes. Sprinkle with cheese.

BAKE for 25 to 30 minutes or until potatoes are tender and cheese is light golden brown.

Makes 8 servings

Shrimp Fettuccine

8 ounces dry fettuccine

1 tablespoon olive oil

2 cloves garlic, finely chopped

2 tablespoons all-purpose flour

⅛ teaspoon ground black pepper

1 cup NESTLÉ® CARNATION® Evaporated Lowfat 2% Milk

¾ cup vegetable or chicken broth

½ cup (1.5 ounces) plus 2 tablespoons shredded Parmesan cheese, *divided*

½ pound cooked medium shrimp

½ cup chopped red bell pepper

Fresh whole or finely sliced basil leaves for garnish (optional)

PREPARE pasta according to package directions; drain.

MEANWHILE, HEAT oil and garlic in medium saucepan over medium heat until garlic is fragrant. Stir in flour and black pepper; cook, stirring constantly, for 30 seconds. Add evaporated milk and broth. Cook, stirring constantly, for about 8 minutes or until mixture comes to a gentle boil and thickens slightly. Stir in *½ cup* cheese until melted. Add shrimp and bell pepper; heat for an additional minute or until shrimp are warm.

TOSS with pasta. Top with *remaining 2 tablespoons* cheese and basil. Serve immediately.

Makes 6 servings

Pumpkin Chili Mexicana

2 tablespoons vegetable oil

½ cup chopped onion

1 cup (1 large) chopped red or green bell pepper

1 clove garlic, finely chopped

1 pound ground turkey

2 cans (14.5 ounces *each*) no-salt-added diced tomatoes, undrained

1 can (15 ounces) LIBBY'S® 100% Pure Pumpkin

1 can (15 ounces) tomato sauce

1 can (15.25 ounces) kidney beans, drained

1 can (4 ounces) diced green chiles

½ cup loose-pack frozen whole kernel corn

1 tablespoon chili powder

1 teaspoon ground cumin

½ teaspoon ground black pepper

HEAT vegetable oil in large saucepan over medium-high heat. Add onion, bell pepper and garlic; cook, stirring frequently, for 5 to 7 minutes or until tender. Add turkey; cook until browned. Drain.

ADD tomatoes with juice, pumpkin, tomato sauce, beans, chiles, corn, chili powder, cumin and black pepper. Bring to a boil. Reduce heat to low. Cover; cook, stirring occasionally, for 30 minutes.

Makes 6 to 8 servings

Simple Risotto with Peas & Parmesan

1 tablespoon olive oil

1 small onion, finely chopped

2 cloves garlic, finely chopped

1 cup uncooked arborio rice

2 cups chicken broth or stock

1 cup **NESTLÉ® CARNATION® Evaporated Lowfat 2% Milk**

½ cup frozen peas, thawed

¼ to ½ teaspoon lemon zest (optional)

Salt and ground black pepper to taste

¼ cup (about 1 ounce) finely shredded Parmesan cheese

HEAT oil in medium, nonstick saucepan over medium-high heat. Add onion; cook, stirring occasionally, for about 3 minutes or until onion is tender. Stir in garlic and cook until aroma is released (do not brown). Stir in rice; cook, stirring frequently, for 1 minute.

STIR in broth and evaporated milk. Reduce heat to medium. Cook, stirring frequently, for 20 to 25 minutes or until rice is tender but firm to the bite (mixture will be creamy and more stirring will be needed as it becomes thicker). Remove from heat; stir in peas and lemon zest. Season with salt and pepper to taste. Serve immediately with Parmesan cheese.

Makes 9 servings

Creamy Cheesy Mashed Potatoes

6 medium (about 2 pounds *total*) potatoes, peeled and cut into 1-inch chunks

¾ cup NESTLÉ® CARNATION® Evaporated Milk

¼ cup (½ stick) butter or margarine

1 cup (4 ounces) shredded cheddar cheese

PLACE potatoes in large saucepan. Cover with water; bring to a boil. Cook over medium-high heat for 15 to 20 minutes or until tender; drain.

RETURN potatoes to saucepan; add evaporated milk and butter. Beat with hand-held mixer until smooth. Stir in cheese. Season with salt and ground black pepper.

NOTE: Chopped green onions, chopped parsley or cooked, crumbled bacon may be added to mashed potatoes.

Makes 6 servings

Pumpkin Curry Soup

- **2 tablespoons butter or margarine**
- **1 cup (1 small) chopped onion**
- **2 large cloves garlic, finely chopped**
- **1½ teaspoons curry powder**
- **½ teaspoon salt**
- **¼ teaspoon ground white pepper**
- **3 cups chicken broth**
- **1 can (15 ounces) LIBBY'S® 100% Pure Pumpkin**
- **1 can (12 fluid ounces) NESTLÉ® CARNATION® Evaporated Milk**

MELT butter in large saucepan over medium-high heat. Add onion and garlic; cook for 2 to 3 minutes or until tender. Stir in curry powder, salt and pepper; cook for 1 minute.

ADD broth and pumpkin; bring to a boil. Reduce heat to low; cook, stirring occasionally, for 15 to 20 minutes. Stir in evaporated milk. Transfer mixture to food processor or blender (in batches, if necessary); cover. Blend until smooth. Serve warm.

Makes 6 servings

Moroccan-Spiced Chicken & Rice Bake

6 cups cooked long or medium grain brown or white rice

1 tablespoon ground cumin

1½ teaspoons salt

1 teaspoon ground black pepper

1½ teaspoons ground paprika

6 chicken thighs, skin removed

2 tablespoons olive oil

3 cloves garlic, finely chopped

1 can (12 fluid ounces) NESTLÉ® CARNATION® Evaporated Milk

1 can (14.5 ounces) petite diced tomatoes, drained

⅔ cup raisins

3 tablespoons lemon juice

½ cup toasted, slivered almonds (optional)

PREHEAT oven 375°F. Grease 13× 9-inch baking dish.

COMBINE cumin, salt, pepper and paprika in small bowl; sprinkle *2 teaspoons* spice blend on both sides of chicken thighs.

HEAT olive oil and garlic in large skillet over medium-high heat. Place chicken in skillet; cook for 4 minutes per side or until browned.

MEANWHILE, COMBINE cooked rice, evaporated milk, tomatoes, raisins, lemon juice and *remaining* spice blend in large bowl. Pour rice mixture into prepared baking dish. Place chicken thighs on top of rice mixture.

BAKE for 40 minutes or until chicken is no longer pink in center. Sprinkle with almonds before serving.

Makes 6 servings

Tip: Boneless chicken thighs can also be used. Reduce bake time by 10 to 15 minutes.

Creamy Chicken and Rice Bake

1 can (12 fluid ounces) NESTLÉ® CARNATION® Evaporated Milk

1 package (3 ounces) cream cheese, softened

1 can (10¾ ounces) cream of chicken soup

½ cup water

½ teaspoon garlic powder

⅛ teaspoon ground black pepper

1 bag (16 ounces) frozen broccoli, cauliflower and carrot mix, thawed

2 cups cubed, precooked chicken

1½ cups uncooked instant white rice

½ cup (2 ounces) shredded mild Cheddar cheese

PREHEAT oven to 350°F. Grease 13×9-inch baking dish.

COMBINE evaporated milk and cream cheese in baking dish with wire whisk until smooth. Add soup, water, garlic powder and pepper; mix well. Add vegetables, chicken and rice. Cover tightly with foil.

BAKE for 35 minutes. Uncover; top with cheese. Bake for an additional 10 to 15 minutes or until cheese is melted and mixture is bubbly. Let stand 5 minutes before serving.

Makes 8 to 10 servings

Chicken Tortilla Stew

4 to 5 cooked, boneless, skinless chicken breast halves or 1 rotisserie chicken, shredded (about 6 cups)

3 cans (14 fluid ounces *each*) reduced sodium chicken broth

2 cans (10 ounces *each*) mild red or green chili enchilada sauce

1 can (12 fluid ounces) **NESTLÉ® CARNATION®** Evaporated Milk

2 cups matchstick or shredded carrots

1 cup uncooked long or medium grain rice

1½ teaspoons ground cumin

2 cups frozen whole-kernel corn, thawed

1½ cups broken tortilla chips

Fresh cilantro leaves, sliced green onions (optional)

COMBINE broth, enchilada sauce, evaporated milk, carrots, rice and cumin in large saucepan. Cook over medium-high heat until mixture begins to simmer. Reduce heat to medium-low. Simmer for 15 to 20 minutes, stirring occasionally, until rice is tender. Add chicken and corn; stir well.

SPOON into serving bowls; top each serving with tortilla chips, cilantro leaves and green onions, if desired.

Makes 9 servings

Tip: Different brands of enchilada sauce may have different heat levels. A hotter enchilada sauce can be used if a spicier stew is desired.

Tip: Freeze half the stew for another meal. Thaw in refrigerator and reheat in microwave or on stovetop.

Creamy Pesto Garden Pasta

1 box (12 ounces) dry tri-color rotini or spiral-shaped pasta

1 bag (16 ounces) frozen broccoli, cauliflower and carrot medley

1 can (12 fluid ounces) NESTLÉ® CARNATION® Evaporated Milk

2 cups (8-ounce package) shredded Italian cheese blend or Monterey Jack cheese

3 tablespoons jarred or refrigerated pesto with basil

¼ teaspoon ground black pepper

2 cups (8 ounces) cooked ham, cut into ½-inch pieces

COOK pasta according to package directions, adding frozen vegetables to boiling pasta water for last 2 minutes of cooking time; drain. Return pasta and vegetables to cooking pot.

MEANWHILE, COMBINE evaporated milk, cheese, pesto and black pepper in medium saucepan. Cook over medium-low heat, stirring occasionally, until cheese is melted. Remove from heat.

POUR cheese sauce over pasta and vegetables. Add ham; stir until combined.

Makes 6 servings

Crustless Broccoli & Cheddar Mini Quiches

1 can (12 fluid ounces) NESTLÉ® CARNATION® Evaporated Lowfat 2% Milk

3 large eggs, beaten

2 tablespoons all-purpose flour

¼ teaspoon salt

¼ teaspoon ground black pepper

2 cups (8-ounce package) shredded mild or sharp Cheddar cheese

2 cups frozen chopped broccoli, thawed and drained

½ cup chopped red bell pepper

PREHEAT oven to 350°F. Grease and lightly flour twelve 2½-inch muffin cups.

WHISK evaporated milk, eggs, flour, salt and black pepper in medium bowl until blended. Stir in cheese, broccoli and bell pepper. Spoon ¼ to ⅓ cup of mixture into each prepared muffin cup, filling almost to rim. Stir mixture frequently to evenly distribute ingredients.

BAKE for 23 to 28 minutes or until knife inserted near centers comes out clean and tops are lightly browned. Cool in pans for 15 minutes. Run knife or small, flat spatula around inside edges of muffin cups. Carefully remove quiches.

Makes 12 servings

Cranberry-Dressed Mixed Greens with Apples & Glazed Pecans

Dressing

⅔ cup (5 fluid-ounce can) NESTLÉ® CARNATION® Fat Free Evaporated Milk

½ cup sweetened dried cranberries

3 tablespoons mayonnaise

3 tablespoons cranberry juice concentrate

2 teaspoons lemon juice

1 small clove garlic, finely chopped (optional)

¼ teaspoon salt

¼ teaspoon ground black pepper

½ teaspoon dried tarragon leaves

Salad

6 cups (about 5.5-ounce bag) mixed baby greens

2 tart apples (such as Granny Smith), cored, diced

½ cup sweetened dried cranberries

½ cup glazed pecans

For Dressing

PLACE evaporated milk, cranberries, mayonnaise, cranberry juice concentrate, lemon juice, garlic, salt and pepper in blender; cover. Blend until combined. Stir in tarragon. Makes 1¼ cups.

For Salad

COMBINE greens, apples, cranberries and *1 cup* dressing in large bowl. Sprinkle with pecans. Serve with remaining dressing, if desired.

Makes 4 servings

Cooking Tip: For a heartier salad, add diced, cooked turkey.

Metric Conversion Chart

VOLUME MEASUREMENTS (dry)

$^1/_8$ teaspoon = 0.5 mL
$^1/_4$ teaspoon = 1 mL
$^1/_2$ teaspoon = 2 mL
$^3/_4$ teaspoon = 4 mL
1 teaspoon = 5 mL
1 tablespoon = 15 mL
2 tablespoons = 30 mL
$^1/_4$ cup = 60 mL
$^1/_3$ cup = 75 mL
$^1/_2$ cup = 125 mL
$^2/_3$ cup = 150 mL
$^3/_4$ cup = 175 mL
1 cup = 250 mL
2 cups = 1 pint = 500 mL
3 cups = 750 mL
4 cups = 1 quart = 1 L

VOLUME MEASUREMENTS (fluid)

1 fluid ounce (2 tablespoons) = 30 mL
4 fluid ounces ($^1/_2$ cup) = 125 mL
8 fluid ounces (1 cup) = 250 mL
12 fluid ounces (1$^1/_2$ cups) = 375 mL
16 fluid ounces (2 cups) = 500 mL

WEIGHTS (mass)

$^1/_2$ ounce = 15 g
1 ounce = 30 g
3 ounces = 90 g
4 ounces = 120 g
8 ounces = 225 g
10 ounces = 285 g
12 ounces = 360 g
16 ounces = 1 pound = 450 g

DIMENSIONS

$^1/_{16}$ inch = 2 mm
$^1/_8$ inch = 3 mm
$^1/_4$ inch = 6 mm
$^1/_2$ inch = 1.5 cm
$^3/_4$ inch = 2 cm
1 inch = 2.5 cm

OVEN TEMPERATURES

250°F = 120°C
275°F = 140°C
300°F = 150°C
325°F = 160°C
350°F = 180°C
375°F = 190°C
400°F = 200°C
425°F = 220°C
450°F = 230°C

BAKING PAN SIZES

Utensil	Size in Inches/Quarts	Metric Volume	Size in Centimeters
Baking or	$8 \times 8 \times 2$	2 L	$20 \times 20 \times 5$
Cake Pan	$9 \times 9 \times 2$	2.5 L	$23 \times 23 \times 5$
(square or	$12 \times 8 \times 2$	3 L	$30 \times 20 \times 5$
rectangular)	$13 \times 9 \times 2$	3.5 L	$33 \times 23 \times 5$
Loaf Pan	$8 \times 4 \times 3$	1.5 L	$20 \times 10 \times 7$
	$9 \times 5 \times 3$	2 L	$23 \times 13 \times 7$
Round Layer	$8 \times 1^1/_2$	1.2 L	20×4
Cake Pan	$9 \times 1^1/_2$	1.5 L	23×4
Pie Plate	$8 \times 1^1/_4$	750 mL	20×3
	$9 \times 1^1/_4$	1 L	23×3
Baking Dish	1 quart	1 L	—
or Casserole	1$^1/_2$ quarts	1.5 L	—
	2 quarts	2 L	—

BAKE THE VERY BEST®

TOLL HOUSE SINCE 1939

Nestlé®

Celebrate the holidays with the N___ family of superb ___! Inside this ___ssic collection of more than 50 recipes, you'll find chip-filled cookies, decadent candies, flavor-packed cakes and pies, savory mealtime dishes, and more. Entertaining during the holiday season has never been more delicious!

Manufactured in China.

06/25/2016 Shanghai
0146757MF4

ISBN-13: 978-1-4508-7075-7
ISBN-10: 1-4508-7075-9

9 781450 870757

Publications International, Ltd.
Morton Grove, IL 60053